Michael Bernays

Madame Dowding's corsets

Michael Bernays

Madame Dowding's corsets

ISBN/EAN: 9783742832580

Manufactured in Europe, USA, Canada, Australia, Japa

Cover: Foto ©Thomas Meinert / pixelio.de

Manufactured and distributed by brebook publishing software (www.brebook.com)

Michael Bernays

Madame Dowding's corsets

DOWDING'S
REJANE

REJANE

MADAME DOWDING,

8 & 10, CHARING CROSS ROAD

LADIES' TAILOR, CORSETIÈRE, and COURT DRESSMAKER.

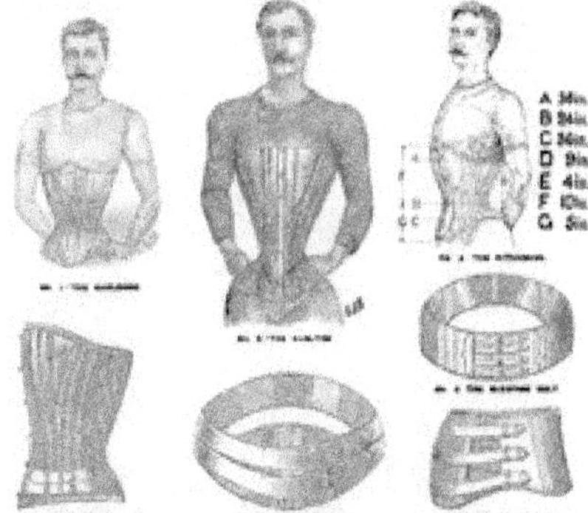

MADAME DOWDING,

8 & 10, CHARING CROSS ROAD.

LADIES' TAILOR, CORSETIERE, and COURT DRESSMAKER.

HUNTING CORSET.

GOLFING.

CYCLING.

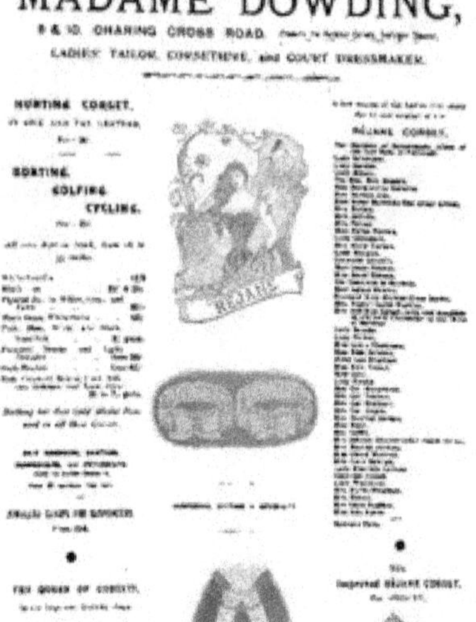

RÉJANE CORSET.

THE QUEEN OF CORSETS.

The Improved RÉJANE CORSET.

MADAME DOWDING.

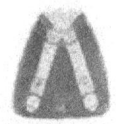

MADAM D——G'S LATEST BELT FOR OBESITY.

"Oh! Madam, this terrible pressure will give me severe indigestion."

"Madam D——g: Hurry up, Joseph, give him some of Buller's Pills, they will soon cure him."

February 5, 1900

CORRESPONDENCE.

To the Editor of "Society."

MADAME DOWDING.

THE DOWDINGNIAN "BEAUTY."

Silk Skirts to match from 30s.

MADAME DOWDING, 8 and 10, CHARING CROSS ROAD.

CORRESPONDENCE

CORSETS FOR MEN

THE PELICAN.
MADAME DOWDING.
MADAME DOWDING,

MADAME DOWDING,
THE IMPROVED RÉJANE CORSET

The "Dowdinian,"
Madame Dowding,

Mrs. Dowding,

CORRESPONDENCE.

The Ladies' Field.

THE LADIES' FIELD
MADAME DOWDING,
MADAME DOWDING,

The Small Waist Competition

has now proved beyond doubt that there is neither a 12-inch nor 13-inch waist in existence, the nearest being

13½-inch—a doctor's wife.

3 . . . 14 inch.

5 . . . 15 inch.

This will answer so many enquiries made on the subject of small waists.

Yours faithfully,

RACHEL DOWDING.

MADAME DOWDING'S
Small Waist Competition,

Open to Every Lady in Great Britain up to and including April 30th, 1909.

[illegible]

THE QUEEN OF CORSETS. [illegible]

MADAME DOWDING,

8 & 10, CHARING CROSS ROAD, [illegible]

MADAME DOWDING,

8 & 10, CHARING CROSS ROAD.

LADIES' TAILOR, CORSETIÈRE, and COURT DRESSMAKER.

THE IMPROVED

Réjane Corset

FOR OBESITY.

INDIVIDUAL FITTING A SPECIALTY.

Butterfly's Answers.

June 28, 1900

The Pelican.

SATURDAY, MAR. 24, 1900.

THE PELICAN.

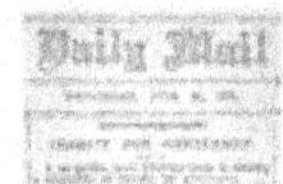
Daily Mail

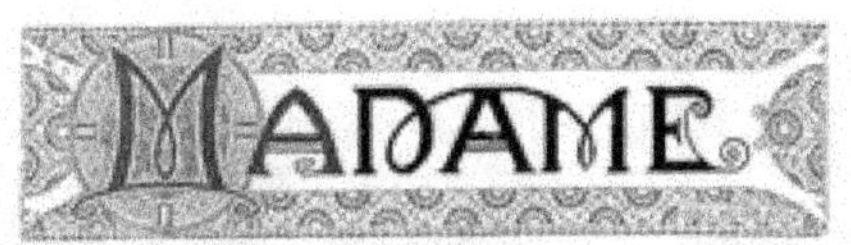

MADAME

No. 236—Vol. XVII. MARCH 10th, 1900. [PRICE 2d.

MADAME DOWDING

The Perfection "Corset"

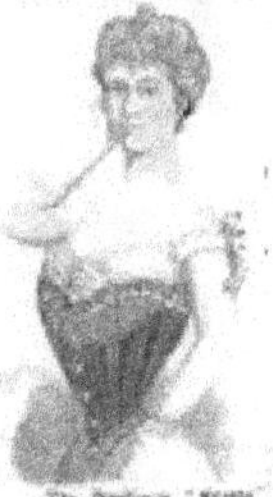

TROCADERO, The Restaurant of the World. Piccadilly Circus, W. ONE PENNY.

THE FREE LANCE

EDITED BY

CLEMENT SCOTT

CONTENTS

No. 1 Vol. 1.

OCTOBER 6, 1900.

The Drama of To-day

Sec. of State, Indian Dept. ....

Secretary for Scotland ....

First Lord of the Admiralty ....

First Lord of the Treasury ....

Lord Lieutenant of Ireland ....

Lord Chancellor of Ireland ....

President of Board of Trade ....

Chancellor of the Duchy of Lancaster ....

President Local Government Board ....

President Board of Agriculture ....

Works and Public Buildings ....

Chief Secretary for Ireland ....

Postmaster-General ....

Civil Lord of the Admiralty ....

Parliamentary Secretary, Home Office ....

" " Foreign Office ....

" " Colonial Office ....

" " India Office ....

" " War Office ....

Attorney-General ....

Solicitor-General ....

Name of Competitor ....

Address ....

NOTE TO CONTRIBUTORS.

The Editor will always be pleased to consider type-written MSS., which, however, will not be returned unless accompanied by a stamped and addressed envelope.

[illegible]
[illegible]
First Lord of the Admiralty
First Lord of the Treasury
Lord Lieutenant of Ireland
Lord Chancellor of Ireland
President of Board of Trade
Chancellor of the Duchy of Lancaster
President Local Government Board
President Board of Agriculture
Works and Public Buildings
[illegible]
Chief Secretary for Ireland
Postmaster General
[illegible]
Parliamentary Secretary, Home Office
" " Foreign Office
" " Colonial Office
" " India Office
" " War Office
Attorney General
Solicitor General
[illegible]
[illegible]

NOTE TO CONTRIBUTORS.

[illegible]

TROCADERO, Piccadilly Circus, W.
ONE PENNY.
THE FREE LANCE
EDITED BY
CLEMENT SCOTT
CONTENTS
OCTOBER 6, 1900.
The Drama of To-day
CLEMENT SCOTT.
Interview with Queen Nathalie.
The Wheel of Life.
"Mainly for Women."
Literature, Art, Music.
Sport, Finance.
All Sorts of Things
Manners! Gentlemen!
MARIE CORELLI.
J. J. CARRERAS,
SCHWEITZER'S COCOATINA.
Schweppes Soda.
SCHWEPPES Mineral Waters.
Schweppes Soda.
LONDON HIPPODROME,
An Entertainment of Unexampled Brilliance

Daily Mail.

FRIDAY, SEPTEMBER

THE SMALLEST WAIST.

Daily Mail.

FRIDAY, SEPTEMBER 2, 1900.

THE SMALLEST MONEY.

Dangers of the Modern Coinage.

The Topical Times

No. [illegible] LONDON, SATURDAY, OCTOBER [illegible] [illegible] ONE PENNY.

SOCIETY.

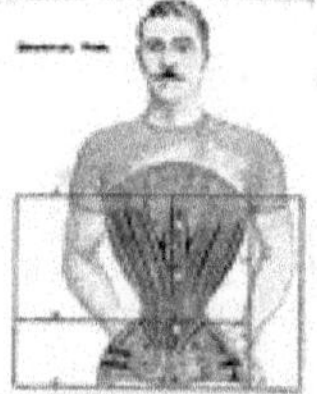

THE "UNIVERSITY."

MADAME DOWDING.

MADAME DOWDING,

8 & 10, Charing Cross Road.

Pelican

SATURDAY, MAR. 31, 1900.

THE LADIES' FIELD

THE "CARLTON."

Mme. Dowding.

Dress and Fashion.

Home Chat.

HOME CHAT

EDITORIAL OFFICE,

[illegible] BUILDINGS,

[illegible] STREET, LONDON, E.C.

8th October, 1906.

[illegible],

The [illegible] recommended by Lady Betty [illegible] [illegible], [illegible] Cross [illegible], London, W.C.

Yours faithfully,

pro The Editress.

[illegible]

October 10, 1906.

[illegible]

Miss Matthews has been recommended by Lady Betty of Home Chat to buy your carpets which are said to be very good. But Miss M. thinks they are very expensive & [illegible]

The
ADVERTISING WORLD
The
ADVERTISING
WORLD
Vol. 5.
No 1.
APRIL
A
JOURNAL
of
NEWS
and
CRITICISMS
for
Published Monthly
COLUMBUS, OHIO.

DOWDING'S
REJANE
CORSET

REJANE

MADAME DOWDING,

8 & 10, CHARING CROSS ROAD,

LADIES' TAILOR, CORSETIERE, and COURT DRESSMAKER.

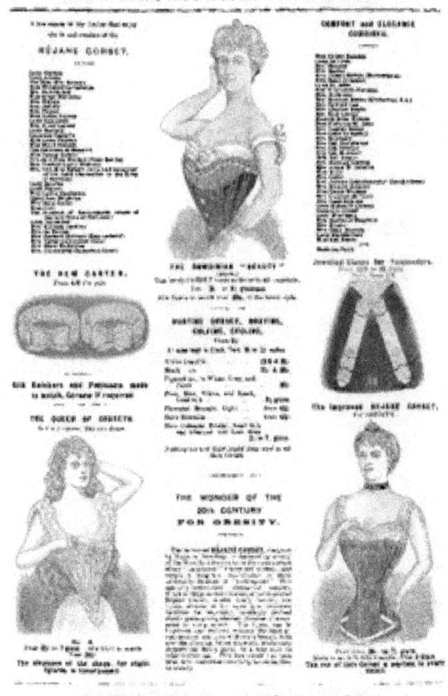

MADAME DOWDING.

MADAME DOWDING.

A few unsolicited Testimonials for the Rejane Corset designed by Madame Dowding.

Hyperion, Liverwood, Torquay.
Dear Madam,—I am glad to tell you my Corsets are very comfortable, and like them extremely.
Yours truly, GERTRUDE SOMERS.

13, Great Stanhope Street, Mayfair, London.
[illegible]

[illegible], Hampstead.
Dear Madame Dowding,—[illegible] Rejane Corsets. [illegible]
Yours sincerely, NINA MARDON (From Berlin).

[illegible] Hall, [illegible], co. Dublin.
[illegible] Rejane Corsets are wonderful, and strongly recommends them for cycling. The shape is perfect.

Cardiff, South Wales.
Lady [illegible] presents her compliments to Madame Dowding, [illegible] Rejane Corset, [illegible]

[illegible] Square.
The [illegible] is delighted with the Rejane Corset; [illegible]

[illegible], Berwick, Sussex.
Dear Madame Dowding,—The Corsets are most satisfactory.
Yours truly, E. H. GAYLAND.

The Lodge, [illegible], Whitby.
Dear Madame Dowding,—[illegible]
Yours truly, EMILY F. SHORT.

[illegible]
Dear Madam,—My Corsets are most comfortable.
Yours truly, A. BEAN.

[illegible], N.B.
[illegible]

The Manor House, [illegible].
Dear Madam,—I am very pleased with my Corsets.
Yours truly, M. GATES.

[illegible] Lodge, Richmond, Surrey.
Dear Madame Dowding,—I am very pleased with my Corsets, [illegible]
Yours truly, L. TANTEN.

The [illegible], Surrey.
[illegible]
Yours truly, ALICE [illegible].

[illegible]
Dear Madam,—The Corsets are quite lovely. [illegible]
Yours truly, KATE CUTLER.

[illegible], Edinburgh.
Corsets received are most satisfactory. E. [illegible]

[illegible], Brighton.
[illegible]

[illegible]
[illegible]
Yours sincerely, FRANCES E. COTTINGHAM.

[illegible], St. Petersburg, Russia.
[illegible]
Yours truly, [illegible].

[illegible], Ireland.
[illegible]

[illegible]
Madame Dowding, [illegible]
Yours truly, A. MARSHALL.

[illegible], Cheshire.
[illegible]
Yours truly, S. W. GIBSON.

[illegible]
[illegible]

[illegible], S. Wales.
[illegible]
Yours faithfully, E. H. [illegible]

[illegible], Hyde Park.
I like my Corsets very much.
Yours faithfully, A. FRANCIS.

[illegible], Hyde Park.
[illegible]

[illegible], W.
My Corsets are very comfortable, [illegible]
Yours truly, EMILY HASTINGS.

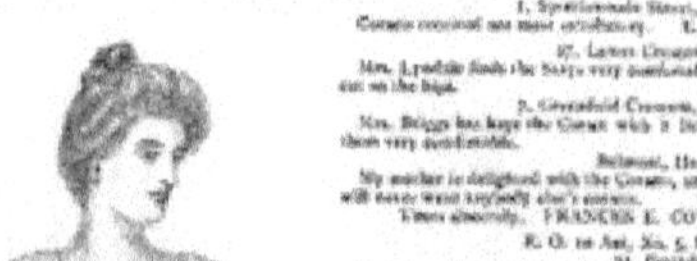

Made to order from 21/-

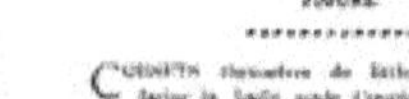

"THE CHARM OF A WOMAN IS HER FIGURE."

CORSETS themselves do little injury, but tight lacing in badly made Corsets is the root of all evil, while a good out stay, rightly [illegible], can do no harm but give **ease, elegance** and **great comfort** to the wearer.

No. 1—THE HUNTING BELT.

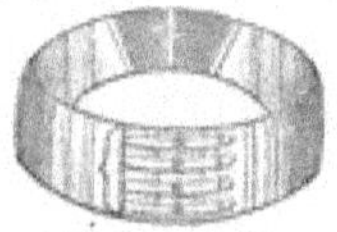

No. 3—THE SLEEPING BELT.

No. 4—THE "UNIVERSITY."

A. Chest, 36 in.
B. Waist, [illegible] in.
C. Hips, 36 in.
D. Under arm to waist, 9 in.
E. Waist to bottom of Belt, 3 in.

INDIVIDUAL FITTING A SPECIALITY.

No. 6—THE CARLTON.

No. 1.—**The Hunting Belt.** Tan Leather, 30/-; Coutille, with Leather [illegible], from 30/-

No. 3.—**The Sleeping Belt.** White and Coloured [illegible], with Elastic [illegible]. The best Belt for [illegible] the Figure, from 21/-

No. 4.—**The University.** A most comfortable shape for day or evening wear, made in all materials, from 30/- to **6 guineas**. Most popular Belt for gentlemen inclined to obesity. [illegible]

No. 6.—**The Carlton.** A great favourite with military gentlemen. Silk Coutille, from 30/-; Black and Coloured [illegible], from 20/-

All these Belts are absolutely Hygienic, and can only be procured from Madame DOWDING, the Sole Inventor and Designer.

No orders can be executed under seven days' notice. [illegible]

All Communications STRICTLY PRIVATE to Belt Department.

CORSETS OF THE HOUR.

The Gentlewoman
The Illustrated Weekly Journal for Gentlewomen
Saturday, October 1903.

Daily Mail

Daily Circulation Five Times as Large as That of Any Penny London Morning Journ[al]

The Daily Mirror

No. 19 — MONDAY, NOVEMBER 23, 1903. — One Penn

Thursday, Dec. 17, 1903.

Madame DOWDING

FOR THE WHOLE WORLD OF WOMEN.

THURSDAY, SEPTEMBER 15, 1904.

ROUND THE SHOPS.

WHAT TO BUY AND WHERE TO BUY IT.

Stanley Dowding

Gentleman's Corset and Belt Specialist.

The Ritz.

THE RITZ.

17, CHARING CROSS RD.

The
Daily Mirror.

COUNTRY LIFE

A CHAT
ABOUT
CORSETS

The Pelican.

A JOURNAL OF TO-DAY.

EDITED BY FRANK M. BOYD.

"Prop all you down, for your are all to then."

No. 854.—Vol. XXXII. SATURDAY DEC. 19, 1903. One Penny.

MADAME DOWDING.

MADAME DOWDING, Costumier,
& 8, 10, Charing Cross Road

FROM THE LADY BEATRIX.

Yours truly, BEATRIX.

❧ CHIC ❧
A High-class Illustrated Ladies' Paper.

No. 45.—Vol. VIII. Saturday, December 12, 1903. [Registered As a Newspaper.]

The "[...]"

AT MADAME DOWNING'S.

[body text illegible]

ÉDITION ANGLAISE PARIS FASHIONS Samedi, Décembre 10, 1904.

LA NOUVELLE MODE

AGENCE ANGLAISE	BUREAU FRANÇAIS
W. J. PATRICK & SONS Ltd. "Self-Reliant" House 47-51, Shoe Street, Shaftesbury Avenue LONDON, W.	3, Boulevard des Capucines, 3 Près le Place de l'Opéra PARIS

MADAME DOWDING, Corsetiere.

8 & 10, Charing Cross Rd.

UNDER ROYAL AND DISTINGUISHED PATRONAGE.

MADAME DOWDING,

The Leading Corsetiere,

8 & 10, CHARING CROSS ROAD, W.C.

No. 5.—
The SLEEPING BELT.
White and Coloured Cloths, with elastic and perforated systems.
The Finest Belt for cultivating the Figure.
From 21/-

No. 1—The CARLTON.

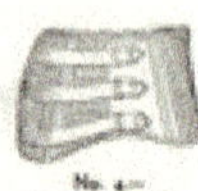

No. 4.—
The GOLF BELT.
Tan Leather, 30/-
Coutille, with Leather Bands, from 30/-

No. 2—The DON

THESE BELTS are absolutely Hygienic, and can only be procured from MADAME DOWDING, the Sole Inventor and Designer.

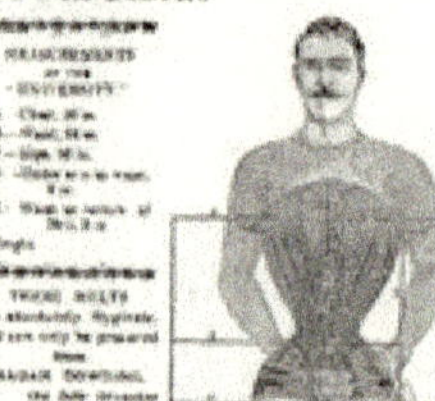

No. 3—The UNIVERSITY

No. 1.—The CARLTON. A great favourite with Military Gentlemen. Silk Coutille from 30/-; Black and Coloured Satins, lined from 30/-.

No. 2.—The DON. White Kid, 30/-; Tan Leather, 33/-, and White Silk Coutille with Kid Straps from 30/-.

No. 3.—The UNIVERSITY. The Latest Invention of Madam Dowding. Made to Order from 2½ Guineas, in Silk Coutille, Satin and perforated Khaki, double run thread, strapped with tan leather.

CHIC

"The Pelican."

The Pelican.

EDITED BY FRANK M. BOYD.

A JOURNAL OF TO-DAY.

MADAME DOWDING.

THE "ELITE."

[illegible]

MADAME DOWDING, [illegible]

[illegible] Charing Cross Road [illegible]

[illegible]

TWO MORE WEEKS!

MADAME

The Leadi

(UNDER ROYAL AND D

"LA FRANCE"

A f

Mdme. Sarah Bernhardt
Vicomtesse [illegible]
Miss Ada Reeve
Comtesse de [illegible]
Lady Mary Sackville
Mrs. Cecil Raleigh
Miss Marie [illegible]
Comtesse de Almeida
Lady Wilkinson
Miss Hilda Moody
Lady Edwards
Comtesse [illegible]
Fraulein Nina [illegible]
Miss Ruth Vincent
Mrs. Charles [illegible]
Mrs. Lewis Waller
Miss Maggie May
Comtesse [illegible]
Miss Clara [illegible]
Lady Cleary
Lady [illegible]
Miss Madie Hope
Miss Hilda Hanbury
Mrs. [illegible]
The Hon'ble. Mrs. [illegible]
Lady Aaron
Miss Muriel Black
Lady [illegible]
Mrs. [illegible]
Mrs. Hilda [illegible]
Miss [illegible]
Miss [illegible]

SHAFTESBURY THEATRE.

SHAFTESBURY AVENUE, W.

Proprietors [illegible] Sole Lessee and Manager ... ... Mr. GEO. MUSGROVE.

To-Night at 8.15, GEORGE MUSGROVE and FRANK McKEE (of New York) introduce

HENRY W. SAVAGE'S AMERICAN COMPANY

In the Musical Comedy, in Two Acts,

THE PRINCE OF PILSEN

Book by FRANK PIXLEY; Music by GUSTAVE LUDERS. Staged by GEORGE MARION.

CAST OF CHARACTERS.

Carl Otto, the Prince of Pilsen, a student of Heidelberg	ROBERT SHOCK
Hans Wagner, a Cincinnati brewer, travelling abroad	JOHN W. RANSONE
Lieut. Tom Wagner, of U.S. Cruiser "Annapolis"	HARRY FAIRLEIGH
Arthur De Willoughby Rosemore, Earl of Shrington, a tourist	VICTOR MORLEY
François, Concierge Hotel Internationale	SHERIDAN WADE
Cook's courier, Vassar Girl's pilot; Sergeant Brie, the Gendarme	MADISON SMITH
Jimmie, a bell boy	EVA WESTCOTT
Mrs. Madison Crocker, from New York	SOPHIE BRANDT
Edith Adams, a Vassar girl	ISABEL HALL
Sidonie, Mrs. Crocker's French maid	EMMA FRANCIS
Nellie Wagner, Hans Wagner's daughter	NANCY MILLS

Rudolph	The Heidelberg Boys	ERNEST HOWELL
Adolph		WILLIAM STEPHENS
Heinrich		LEOPOLD M. LEFFERSON
Fritz		H. B. WHITNEY
Ludwig		CHARLES WILSON
Carl		T. HENRY COOTE
Oscar		FRANK RANDALL
Wilhelm		JOHN HALL
Frankie Frisbie, San Francisco	The American Girls	MABEL WILSON
Dollie Dixie, New Orleans		FLORENCE HOLMES
Priscilla, Plymouth, Boston		MOLLY MACRATH
Penny Penn, Philadelphia		ETHEL CLIFTON
Missy River, St. Louis		IDA STANHOPE
Bin Noyes, Chicago		MABEL SPENCER
Olive Oriole, Baltimore		BESSIE FRAGANZA
Goldie Dome, Washington		NELLIE ADAMS
Maria Manhattan, New York		CAMILLE CLIFFORD
Britannia		MARIE FOLLETTE
Sea Allure	Making the Grand Tour	ETHEL GREY
Pleasant Days		MILDRED KEARNEY
Charming Types		HATTIE WATERS
Lottie Towers		CAROLINE LILJA
White Caps	The Sea Shell Girls	META CALDWELL
Pacific Beach		JANNE PATISON
Woodie Sea		BERTHA BALLOU
Dainty Dolphin		LILLIAN HOLLIS
Birdie Petrel		MARGUERITE SCANLAN
Coralie Shell		KATHLEEN HAMILTON
Lottie Pagge		BETHA ENGLE
Pleasant Tayle		JULIA BLANCHE
Nettie Deep		CARRIE DEMING
Ocean Waters		IRENE ZIPSY
Foamie Crest		GERTRUDE WATKINS
Garnet	The Bathing Girls	SHEBA KAUFFMAN
Emerald		FLORIDA MELAIRE
Amethyst		JENNIE DRUSSE
Opal		FLORENCE HENGELA
Sapphire		VESTA HENGELA
Coral		CARTER MITCHELL
Pearl		MAE HUNTINGTON
Cameo		MAUDE WATKINS
Agate		LELIA SMITH
Diamond		MABEL KENT
Cornelian		ANITA MERIK
Topaz		ELEANORE HENGELA
Vidocq	The Gendarmes	CHARLES SULLIVAN
Sherlock		FRANK IRELAND
Hawkshaw		HERBERT HANSON
Carter		STANLEY DAMERELL

Flower Girls, Naval Cadets, Fox Hunters, French Maids, Waiters, etc.

SYNOPSIS OF SCENERY.

ACT I.—Garden of Hotel Internationale. Afternoon. ACT II.—Court of Hotel Internationale. The next morning.

MUSICAL SYNOPSIS.

[illegible]

The Scenery and Floral Decorations have been rendered Fire Resisting by the Process of The Non-Flammable Wood and Fabrics Co., Ltd., [illegible], Fulham, S.W.

FOR HENRY W. SAVAGE.

Manager ... A. H. CANBY | Stage Director ... CHARLES SINCLAIR | Musical Director ... Mr. EDWARD JONES

Business Manager ... Mr. OSCAR BARRETT, Jun.

PRICES OF ADMISSION.—[illegible]

MATINEE EVERY WEDNESDAY AND SATURDAY AT 2.15.

[illegible]

H. CLAVERIE ET CIE.

XL American Dentifrices

TEOFANI'S

ELECTRIC LIGHT CURE

ELECTRIC BATHS

NURSE STRIDE

ORIGINAL CREATIONS in EVENING TOILETTES

PARIS—242, Rue de Rivoli.

REDFERN

PARIS MODELS in DRESS OF ALL KINDS

LONDON—26 & 27, Conduit St.

DALY'S THEATRE

Mr. GEORGE EDWARDES.

THE CINGALEE

By JAMES T. TANNER.

Music by LIONEL MONCKTON.

Lyrics by ADRIAN ROSS and PERCY GREENBANK

HAWES CRAVEN

Cast of the Play.

QUEEN'S HOTEL AND RESTAURANT

Leicester Square.

Choice Cooking

Charming Orchestra

MADAME DOWDING

THE CIGARETTE OF DISTINCTION, THE NEW 'CRAVEN'

CARRERAS, Ltd.

MADAME DOWDING,

The Leading Corsetiere.

LA FRANCE

THE QUEEN

⋅⋅⋅ THE CHARM OF A WOMAN IS HER FIGURE. ⋅⋅⋅

Tight Lacing in badly made Corsets is the root of all evil, while a good cut Stay, tightly braced, can do no harm, but give Ease, Elegance, and great comfort to the wearer.

⋅⋅ Individual Fitting a Speciality. ⋅⋅

FARADAY HOUSE, 8 & 10, CHARING CROSS ROAD.

MADAME DOWDING.

STOUT FIGURES

can easily obtain a Straight Front below the waist by wearing

Madame DOWDING'S CORSETS.

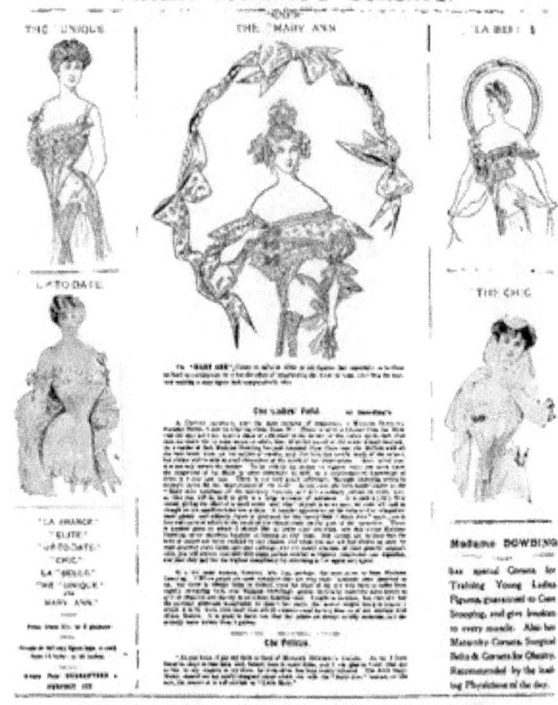

FARADAY HOUSE, 8 & 10, CHARING CROSS ROAD.

OPINIONS OF THE PRESS

THE SECRET OF THE WASP WAIST.

CHAT WITH A CORSETIERE.

Stays that Cost Ten Guineas Apiece.

A few of Madame Dowding's Clienteles.

The Favourite

BADEN-BADEN

Natural
Mineral Water.

At the Bars of this Theatre

CUCKOO CLOCKS,

Watches, Jewellery,

CLOCKS.

LONDON, W.C.

Madam DOWDING

MERRYWEATHER'S

THREE GREAT SPECIALITIES:-

WATER SUPPLY
TO MANSIONS

FIRE PROTECTION
OF MANSIONS

SAFE
ELECTRIC LIGHTING

MERRYWEATHER'S.

63, LONG ACRE, W.C.

Madame DOWDING

The ASCOT PET

Straight-fronted

SILK SKIRTS

Charing Cross Road.

Alhambra Theatre,

THE NATIONAL THEATRE OF VARIETIES.

PROGRAMME

1\. OVERTURE

2\. The Popular Ballet, entitled

"All the Year Round"

8\. ORCHESTRAL SELECTION

7\. TEN-ICHI TROUPE,

THE "Entente Cordiale."

10\. Tenor.

11\. THE THREE BOGANNYS. 11.10

"The Crazy Bakers."

The Favourite
BADEN-BADEN
Natural
Mineral Water.
At the Bars of this Theatre
CUCKOO CLOCKS,
Watches, Jewellery,
CLOCKS.
Camerer, Kuss & Co.,
LONDON, W.C.
Madam DOWDING
"LA FRANCE"
MERRYWEATHER'S
THREE GREAT SPECIALITIES:-
WATER SUPPLY
TO MANSIONS
FIRE PROTECTION
OF MANSIONS
SAFE
ELECTRIC LIGHTING
MERRYWEATHER'S,
63, LONG ACRE, W.C.
The ASCOT PET
Straight-fronted
Madam Dowding,
Charing Cross Road.

LONDON HIPPODROME,

CRANBOURN STREET, LEICESTER SQUARE, W.C.

(Designed by FRANK MATCHAM, Architect.)

Proprietors - MOSS' EMPIRES LIMITED (Total Capital, £1,400,000).
Managing Director - - - - - - - Mr. H. E. MOSS
General Manager - - - - - Mr. FRANK ALLEN

TWICE DAILY at 2 and 7-45 O'CLOCK.

PROGRAMME.

1—OVERTURE

2—Mdlle. GERTRELLA, assisted by ELSIE, Speciality Act, "In Cupid's Garden"

3—BOSWELL'S MINIATURE CIRCUS.

4—ALEXANDER and HUGHES Musical Comedians

5—PAUL COURTAULT - Novelty Jockey Act

6—MORRIS CRONIN AND TROUPE Modern Jugglers

7—SELECTION

8—SALAMONSKY - - with his Fire Horse

9—FRANCIS WYLIE - Original Dog Act

10—MARCELINE - - - The Droll

11—CARL HERTZ - Illusionist and Conjurer

12—GRIFFITHS BROTHERS The Favourite Burlesque Comedians

13—THE KELLINOS In their Speciality Act, "VENETIA"

14—NEWHOUSE AND WARD - Trick Cyclists

15—

"SIBERIA"

A Sensational Dramatic Incident.

Adapted by W. H. RISQUE.
Music Composed and Arranged by GEORGES JACOBI.

Produced by FRANK PARKER,
INTRODUCING THE

HIPPODROME'S FAMOUS STUD OF PLUNGING HORSES

CAST.

[illegible]

Officers, Soldiers, Citizens, Siberian Exiles, &c., &c., &c.

Scene 1 - - Café in Siberian Military Town

Scene 2 - - - - The Road to the Mines

Scene 3 - - - - - The Frozen River

N.B.—Owing to the elaborate nature of the Programme, which has to be constantly varied, it is impossible for the numbers to run consecutively.

EQUESTRIAN AND STAGE DIRECTOR - - - - MR. FRANK PARKER.
Acting Manager - - - - - Mr. FRED TRUSSELL.
Grand Orchestra of 40 Performers, under the Direction of Mr. CLARENCE C. CORRI.
Ring Master, Mr. OTHO TWIGG. Chief Engineer, Mr. H. W. HAWKINS.
Press Representative - Mr. HENRY W. GARRICK. Advertising Manager - Mr. FRANK ROGERS.

[illegible]

DOORS OPEN at 1-30 and 7-30 p.m. OVERTURE at 2 and 7-45 p.m.

DALY'S THEATRE

UNDER THE MANAGEMENT OF

Mr. GEORGE EDWARDES.

By command of the Lord Chamberlain, the proscenium safety curtain is lowered daily in the presence of the audience, about the middle of the performance, so as to ensure the arrangements being in proper working order.

To-night and every evening at 8, Matinee every Saturday at 2, a New Musical Play in Two Acts, entitled:

THE CINGALEE

OR, SUNNY CEYLON.

By JAMES T. TANNER.

Music by LIONEL MONCKTON.

Lyrics by ADRIAN ROSS and PERCY GREENBANK. Additional Dialogue Lyrics and Numbers by PAUL RUBENS.

Act 1—Vereker's Tea Plantation, "Karagama," Ceylon
Act 2—Boobhamba's Palace by the Lake at Kandy
} By HAWES CRAVEN

The Dances and the Chorus Business and effects arranged by WILLIE WARDE.

The Costumes designed by PERCY ANDERSON.

Costumes by Miss Fisher, B. J. Simmons & Co., and Mrs. Nettleship. Millinery by Madame Adelaide, 21, Wigmore St.

Electrical Engineer, C. Saunders. Machinist, H. Skelton.

Stage Manager ... Mr. J. A. E. MALONE.
Musical Director ... Mr. HOWARD TALBOT.

Fee for this Programme 6d

BOX OFFICE (Mr. [illegible]) OPEN DAILY from 10 till 10.

Private Boxes £1 11s. 6d. to £5 5s.; Orchestra Stalls, 10s. 6d.; Balcony Stalls, 7s. 6d.; Upper Circle (Front Row), 5s.; Other Rows, 4s.; (Unreserved) Pit 2s. 6d.; Gallery, 1s.

Cast of the Play.

HARRY VEREKER	(A Tea Planter)	Mr. C. HAYDEN COFFIN
BOOBHAMBA	(A Noble of Kandy)	Mr. RUTLAND BARRINGTON
SIR PETER LOFTUS	(High Commissioner and Judge, Ceylon)	Mr. FRED KAYE
MYAMGAH	An Indian Servant	Mr. WILLIE WARDE
BOBBY WARREN	Pupils of Vereker on the Tea Plantation.	Mr. W. LOUIS BRADFIELD
DICK BOSANQUET		Mr. CONWAY DIXON
FREDDIE LOWTHER		Mr. ARTHUR HOPE
JACK CLINTON		Mr. ARCHIE ANDERSON
WILLIE WILSON		Mr. J. BODDY
CAPTAIN OF THE GUARD		Mr. NORMAN GREENE
ATTENDANT		Mr. F. J. BLACKMAN
AND		
CHAMBHUDDY RAM	(A Dubas Lawyer)	Mr. HUNTLEY WRIGHT
NANOYA	(A Cingalese Girl)	Miss SYBIL ARUNDALE
PEGGY SABINE		Miss GRACIE LEIGH
NAITOOMA	Four Tea Girls on Vereker's Plantation.	Miss CARRIE MOORE
SAYTAMBI		Miss ALICE D'ORME
MYCHELLAH		Miss FREDA VIVIAN
COORONE		Miss A. HATTON
ANGY LOFTUS	(Sir Peter's Daughter)	Miss DORIS STOCKER
MISS PINKERTON	Angy's Governesses.	Miss NINA SEVENING
FRAULEIN WEINER		Miss PATIENCE SEYMOUR
SIGNORINA TASSO		Miss TOPSY SINDEN
MADEMOISELLE CHIC		Miss MABEL HIRST
AND		
LADY PATRICIA VANE		Miss ISABEL JAY

Solo Dance by Miss TOPSY SINDEN
The Pandora Dance by the SISTERS AMARANTH
Devil Dancing by Mr. WILLIE WARDE.

Business Manager for Mr. George Edwardes ... Mr. G. E. MINOR.

FROM THE LADY HEATHER.

THE CULTURE OF THE FIGURE.—HOW THESE CHANGES OF SHAPE ARE ARRIVED AT.—THE WELL CORSETTED WOMAN.—THE CONCEALMENT OF TOO MUCH PLUMP.

MY DEAR MAUDE,—

"It is really very fatiguing," said a certain lady to her dressmaker when told that her figure was well enough for last year's fashions, but would not do at all for those of this season.

"Isn't it enough that I have to cast aside my gowns as they go out of fashion each year, without being compelled to change my figure?"

Yet that is really what it amounts to. The standards of to-day require that a woman's form should be so totally changed, that her last year's frock will not fit her. She must be wasp-like of waist with trim, not too large hips and figure only slightly enlarging to the bust line.

"The glass of fashion and the mould of form" have altered radically within three or four years and the feminine form is so far from being what it used to be that dressmakers have had to revise their measurements.

Directions, therefore, were given that it was to be lifted, and the straight front corset strapped carefully down by garters to keep the surplus flesh elevated. Apparently it disappeared, but in reality it only changed location. Some of it was added to the waist, although the advocates of the orthodox, original straight front refuse to admit that. However, there are the dressmakers' measurements, which prove conclusively that the size of the waist has increased in the last four years from one to two inches, and in some cases more. Fortunately, the development of the diaphragm, chest, and shoulders has maintained the proportions so that the larger waist has not been so conspicuous as it would have been under other conditions.

Which observations naturally bring me to Madame Dowding, the famous corsetière who has made a deep study of the subject I have been writing about and whose fame is literally world-wide. Those of my readers who are still in town but are on the eve of flight should make a point of visiting Faraday House ere they start. Madame Dowding has ideas, and those who love really pretty and tasteful things—and what woman does not—will find her of great help in making suggestions, especially in the matter of wedding things, equipment for yachting, and so on. When one is at a country place miles from anywhere it is difficult, if not impossible, to obtain one's corsets, petticoats, and so on without fearful delay, and to the woman who loves to look smart even when rusticating a few hours of this sort of thing is so much purgatory. Therefore take my advice, overhaul your trunks before you start and if there is any deficiency hie you to Faraday House, 8 and 10, Charing Cross Road (almost opposite the National Portrait Gallery), and see that the blank is filled by the good fairy, Dowding.

Yours ever,

HEATHER.

THE . . .

LONDON WELSHMAN

Cymro Llundain.

With which is Incorporated the "LONDON KELT."

MADAME DOWDING.

MADAME DOWDING, Corsetiere,

The Pelican.

FROM THE LADY HEATHER.

A Good Time Coming.—The Money Comes From the City.—Lady Curzon's Recovery.—Mrs. Brown Potter's Latest Fiasco.—Black Kid and White Stbaw.—A New Corset.

[body text illegible]

SATURDAY, OCT. 8, 1904.

MADAME DOWDING,

[advertisement text largely illegible]

CHIC

THE LADY'S PAPER.

No. 156.—Vol. XI. Saturday, October 8, 1892. [Price, 1d.

AT DOWDING'S.

The value of consulting our "Leading Costumiers" are so far acknowledged...

MADAME DOWDING,

The Leading Corsetiere.

[Under Royal and Distinguished Patronage.]

THE REDINGOTE

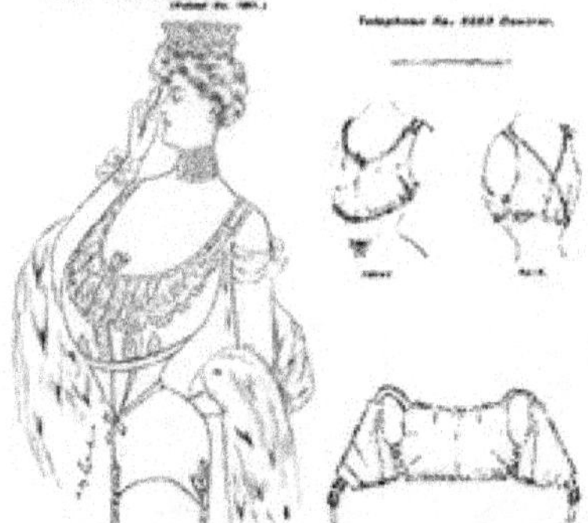

THE CHARM OF A WOMAN IS HER FIGURE.

Price, in Plain Net and Batiste, from 3/6.

Trimmed with Lace and Insertion, from 12/6.

FARADAY HOUSE, 8 & 10, CHARING CROSS ROAD

The Pelican.

SATURDAY, MAR. 28, [illegible]

FROM THE LADY HEATHER.

[illegible]

Yours ever, HEATHER.

LONDON & PARIS
DRESS EXHIBITION

Madam Dowding
Corsetière
17 Charing Cross Road, London, WC

COUNTRY LIFE

The Standard.

LONDON, MONDAY, FEBRUARY 10, 1908. TWELVE PAGES

THE CROWN

No. LXXXII., Vol. I. No. 5. FEBRUARY 1st, 1908. Price One Shilling

The London and Paris Gem Exhibitions

THE LADIES FIELD SUPPLEMENT

THE COURT AND COUNTY FAMILIES NEWSPAPER.

[illegible]

No. LXXXIV., Vol. [illegible], No. [illegible] [illegible] FEBRUARY [illegible] [illegible] Price One Shilling.

or
MADAME DOWDING
MADAME DOWDING, *Court Corsetiere,*
CHARING CROSS ROAD, LONDON, W.C.

Hearth & Home

www.ingramcontent.com/pod-product-compliance
Lightning Source LLC
Chambersburg PA
CBHW031454270326
41930CB00007B/997

* 9 7 8 3 7 4 2 8 3 2 5 8 0 *